MAP YOUR BUSINESS

Define Success, Set Goals, And Make
a Plan (You'll Actually Stick With)

Tara Swiger

Added Bonus Publications
902 E Holston Ave
Johnson City, TN 37601

First softcover edition January 2017

Cover and interior design by Jay Swiger

Names: Swiger, Tara
Title: Map Your Business : Define success, set goals, and
make a plan (you'll actually stick with)

ISBN 978-0-9985571-0-6
ISBN 978-0-9985571-1-3 (e-book)

For the Starship Captains who bravely chart a course,
define success for themselves, and share it all with me.

Thank you.

TABLE OF CONTENTS

"The big question is whether you are going to be able to say a hearty yes to your adventure."
-Joseph Campbell

WELCOME TO YOUR VERY OWN BUSINESS MAP!

You are about to create your own map, for where you want to go in your creative business. You're going to discover where you are, where you want to be, and then create turn-by-turn directions to get there.

While we start with reviewing last year and planning for this one, it's my hope that the chart will be a tool that serves you throughout the year as you learn, change your mind, and dream up fresh new destinations. It can be a living document that you update monthly (or even daily!) with your income goals, planned products, and production schedule.

IT DOESN'T MATTER WHAT THE CALENDAR SAYS.

Whether you're cracking this book open on January 1st or June 3rd or September 29th, it is always the right time to get orientated, get clear, and make a plan. When you read "last year," you can think of the last calendar year, or the previous 12 months in your business; there is no "right" way to make your own map.

The BEST way to make all your dreams come true?

1. Get clear on what you really want.
2. Break it down into do-able steps.
3. Tell someone who can hold you gently, non-guiltily accountable.
4. Reassess and adjust regularly.

THIS BOOK WILL GUIDE YOU THROUGH #1-2, AND PROVIDE YOU WITH TOOLS TO DO #4.

But it cannot, will not, make your dreams come true. You have to put in the effort of getting clear, making a plan and then actually following through and doing the work!

WHAT'S INCLUDED:

* ★ A review of last year
* ★ Plotting your North Star
* ★ Planning exploration for this year
* ★ Monthly reviews + planners to be filled out every month

* Worksheets, lists and prompts to help you remember (and plan for) everything that's coming up
* Map Making process, that guides you to break down your goals into doable steps.

THIS GUIDE WILL LEAD YOU TO:

* Orient yourself in where you are right now
* Define your success
* Shape your coming year around your own landscape
* Create a doable plan that you can readjust as necessary

After you get orientated in where you are right now, set goals for the next year and then make a map (where we break a single goal down into steps), you'll find Monthly Reviews - where you can track your progress and make adjustments. (You don't want to wait until the end of the year before you realize you're not going in the direction you wanted!)

Do it alone and together.

Answer these questions for yourself, but don't keep it to yourself! Ask your partner, kids, and friends what they

have learned, what they want, and make a plan to make
it happen together!

HONOR THE UNIQUE UNIVERSE OF YOUR OWN BUSINESS BY COMMITTING TO NOTICING IT, CHARTING IT, AND FOLLOWING YOUR OWN PATH THROUGH IT.

The principle underlying everything in your roadmap is
simple: Your business is unique. You are unique. You
need to find a way to go about reaching your goals and
dreams in a way that suits you, or you won't stick with it.

With that in mind, use this guide in whatever way works
for you:
* write in it
* make copies
* skip questions that don't suit you
* fill it out forwards or backwards

OPEN IT UP, POUR A CUP OF SOMETHING WARM, AND START WORKING!

* Start with Get Oriented, so you go into the coming
  year with a healthy dose of reality and hope from last

year. But then, go in whatever order you like: skip what doesn't apply and expand on what does.

★ Add in pages from other planners, books, classes, or calendars.

★ If you're into dreamboards, create one every year, month, or quarter and include it in your book.

★ If you're more artist than writer, draw your answers.

★ If you can't think of an answer, make a mind-map.

★ Use pens, markers, stickers, highlighters, paint, fun paper or stitching to make this book as you-filled as you like.

★ Add in anything you learn, think about, or want to study.

★ Keep it on hand so you can add stuff to it when you're inspired.

In other words... make this yours!

GET ORIENTED

Before we look back or look ahead, let's get oriented into where you are right now. (This isn't just about last year, but about your whole life.)

Where are you, right now, in your business and life journey?

What have you overcome?

What challenges do you see ahead?

Where you are is perfect. But everyone has things they thought would happen by now, or things they wish would have worked out differently.

Go on and write down where you WISH you were or where you THOUGHT you'd be.

What about your current situation are you grateful for?

Everything that's come before has led you here. How has it prepared you for what's ahead?

DRAW YOUR UNIVERSE

Let's look at what is your life right now. Draw a mind-map that includes all the parts of your life: your relationships, day-to-day, the spaces you go, the people you talk to. Include your assets – your skills, ideas, dreams... everything that makes your life **your** life. (Not sure how? Instructions: taraswiger.com/mindmap)

Look at what you drew - this is the web that supports you in everything you do. Take a moment to bring each area to mind and feel gratitude for how it supported you last year.

DRAW YOUR BUSINESS UNIVERSE

Let's look at what your business actually is. Draw a mind-map that includes all the parts of your business: your products, sales channels (shops, website, etc), customers, marketing channels, supporters, experience, mentors, assets... everything that makes your business your business.

No matter how big (or small) your business is, it has a universe including your skills, network, and dreams.

Look back at it - this is the web that supports your business in everything you do. Take a moment to bring each area to mind and feel gratitude for how it supported you last year.

What do you want to add to your universe?

What area could use more support or another branch (another shop, a new communication channel, etc.)?

WHAT'S A TYPICAL DAY?

Below, list what a usual day of working in your biz looks like. If you have different kinds of days (admin days, dyeing days), make a different list for each kind of day. (If you work a day job (or night job!) just start your list wherever you start your work. If you only work on weekends, start there!)

What do you like about this?

What do you want to change?

How do you currently track your gross and net income and expenses? (How often and using what?)

What do you like about this? *(If anything!)*

What do you want to change?

What new thing would you like to track?
(Craft show profits? Wholesale profits? Production?
Words written per day or week? Newsletter
subscribers?)

If you have the numbers handy, go ahead and put the
current number here:
(Newsletter subscribers, monthly traffic to your website,
whatever.)

What would you like to plan and schedule in a new
way?
(expenses, production, shipping, daily or weekly projects,
etc.)

CASTING OFF
FROM LAST
YEAR

What did you accomplish last year? Include **everything**, both big and little!

(*Leave space under each one, and take up the next page too!*)

LOOK BACK AT YOUR LIST
OF ACCOMPLISHMENTS

Go back and fill in:

How did you feel when you reached each of those accomplishments?

What surprised you?

(ex. how it happened, when it happened, results you weren't expecting)

THE SECRET OF MY SUCCESS

Go back through your list of accomplishments and look for an underlying theme or lesson.

If you were writing a story titled The Secret of My Success, what would it include? Write it below:

LESSONS LEARNED

What lessons did you learn about yourself last year?

What lessons did you learn about your business?

What specific lessons do you want to bring with you into the next adventure?

GRATITUDE

List what you are/were grateful for.
(*Write, draw, mind-map, collage*)

REMEMBERING THE GOOD

What were some of your favorite moments of the last year?

What challenged you?

How did you spend your time?

What are you proud of?

What did you do that made your life better?

Who was significant in your life?

What did you LOVE last year?

What will you be glad to leave behind?

What do you want to remember?

What do you wish to celebrate?

RELEASING THE MEH

What didn't work for you last year?

What was crazy-making? Ineffective? Frustrating?

What easy solutions do you see, to what didn't work?
(It's ok if there isn't an obvious solution yet, just list what
you see/think might work.)

WORDS

Did you pick a word for last year? If so, write it here:

If not, think back through your year, what word sums up everything?

Last Year was the year of...

NOW THINK BACK THROUGH YOUR YEAR WITH THIS WORD IN MIND.

Write down all the ways you encountered this quality through your year (lessons, experiences, conversations).

THE REAL MONEY STUFF

Now it's time to get specific! If you haven't already, take a break and go total up your sales and expenses.

Then get a tasty beverage and come back for the next section.

What were your gross sales last year?
(The total money you took in, before fees and expenses. You can count anything you want to count - whatever seems like your business to you.)

NOW, TAKE A MINUTE TO CELEBRATE THIS NUMBER!

Even if it looks teeny in comparison to what you wanted, if it's above $0 you are **already** a success at building a business that makes something that people want to buy! *Yay!*

What were your business expenses?
(Count whatever counts for you - supplies, fees, shipping, computer, website hosting.)

What was your net income?
(Take the gross income and subtract the expenses.)

What were your 3 best-selling products?
(And if you sell a lot of colors or styles, what were the top-grossing ones?)

What surprises you about the money stuff?

What lessons can it teach you?

What do you want to remember about the money stuff and bring into the next year?

Anything you need to write/think about before you feel complete with last year?

IT'S TIME TO RELEASE THE MISTAKES AND PAIN IN THE LAST YEAR.

This isn't that fun, but listing and then destroying regrets is a way to acknowledge that you see the pain and that you're ready to be done with it.

List everything that you regret in the last year (harsh words, bad decisions, anything that you don't feel awesome about, big or small)

Now rip this page out of your book and shred it or wad it up and throw it ceremoniously in the trash. Or light it on fire! It's important that you remove it from your life today (don't keep it around to stew over).

Is there anything on the list you didn't feel ready to release?

Write about it, including some steps that might bring you closer to closure.

RELEASE IT ALL

You've found the good, the bad, the lessons and real money-stuff. Now it's time to let it go + accept that this year is going to be different.

No matter what happened last year, a whole new batch of things are going to happen, change, and shift. You will transform. You have already transformed! You are not the same person who went through last year.

This exercise will help you fully process this. By breathing deeply, you kickstart your parasympathetic response, which is a fancy way of saying: you **let your body know it can relax - that it's safe and taken care of.**

Take three deep breaths

Feel your body. Feel where you're sitting, and how supported you are, at this very minute.

TAKE ANOTHER DEEP BREATH

As you take it in, feel around your body. Are you tense anywhere? If so, direct the breath there. Breathe into that tenseness until it starts to release.

TAKE ANOTHER BREATH

RELEASE LAST YEAR
(If you don't know where to start, just breathe into your belly, and on the out breath, say: *I release last year*.)

INVITE IN THE NEW YEAR
(Breathe in: I welcome you, new year.)

TAKE A FEW MORE BREATHS
Notice anything that doesn't feel released. As you breathe out, let it go.

WHEN YOU'RE DONE, REST
Drink a big glass of water.
Lay down, under covers.

Let yourself rest + think about the new year and all the possibilities.

You've done a lot. You've processed a lot. You're allowed to rest.

LAUNCHING
INTO THE NEW

BRING IN THE OLD GOOD

The New Year is new + shiny + exciting! But you found quite a bit of good in your last year, so before we jump into the New, let's bring all the Old Good into the new! Go back through the last year worksheets and copy any of the good bits from last year (or things you want to bring with you) here:

BIG PICTURE-Y

I like to start thinking about the New Year in the most big picture-y way possible, so that we set goals that are in line with what we really want: how we want to feel, how we want to spend our time, and what we want to create.

What do you value?
(in life, in yourself, in others)

How would you like to feel, every day, if you got to choose?

What are the qualities or values you want to see or express in your life?

What do you want to experience?

Who do you want to become?

THIS YEAR

How do you want to feel this year?

What do you want to invite into your life this year?

What would you like to learn?

What's one thing you'd love to accomplish?

Is there a word or phrase that keeps coming to you?

What do you want to be celebrating next December?

FIND YOUR NORTH STAR(S)

Go back through the last three worksheets and look for connections. What seems to really matter to you, based only on the answers you've given? Where is your focus?

List the connections or repeating themes here:

Is anything that is truly important to you missing from the list?

THESE ARE YOUR NORTH STARS
(Yes, you're allowed to have more than one). These are the things that truly matter to you and thus, these are the things that should influence all your planning - **they guide what you do and how you do it.**

For the rest of the book (and the rest of the year), keep your North Star in mind - use it to double check everything:

* Will this lead me towards {my North Star}?
* Is this in integrity with what matters most?
* Is this the most {North Star-like} way to do this?

LONG TERM
AWESOMENESS

This is the place to get big and crazy. We'll make these do-able in the coming pages, so don't worry about that right now.

IN 5 YEARS I'D LIKE TO:

IN 4 YEARS I'D LIKE TO:

IN 3 YEARS I'D LIKE TO:

IN 2 YEARS I'D LIKE TO:

IN 1 YEAR I'D LIKE TO:

THIS WILL BE THE THE
YEAR OF...

This year!

Tell the story of the coming year. Paint a picture (with words or with art!) that includes personal, financial, business, relationships, family, spiritual stuff. Imagine the awesomest version of this coming year + tell it as if it already happened. (Imagine you're telling a very interested friend at the end of the year.)

WHAT DO YOU WANT TO DO OR ACCOMPLISH THIS YEAR?

(List everything, big and little)

Look over your list and find the big 3 or 4 things that are most important - the things that matter most or symbolize other, smaller goals.

Put one at the top of each of the following pages, and then write about it. Include lists of what can get you there (people, to-dos, events) and any ideas you have. (We'll work these out in detail during map-making.)

BEAUTIFUL THING #1

Why do you want to do this?
(What will it bring into your life? What makes you
enthusiastic about it? How is it in line with your North
Star?)

What resources and support do you already have for
this?
(Count everything! Things you already know, people you
can talk to, customers who want this...)

How do you think you'll feel when you accomplish this?
Be specific!

Off the top of your head, what will this involve?
(We'll work these details out during map-making.)

AMAZING THING #2

_____

Why do you want to do this?
(What will it bring into your life? What makes you
enthusiastic about it? How is it in line with your North
Star?)

What resources and support do you already have for
this?
(Count everything! Things you already know, people you
can talk to, customers who want this...)

How do you think you'll feel when you accomplish this?
Be specific!

Off the top of your head, what will this involve?
(*We'll work these details out during map-making.*)

DIVINE THING #3

Why do you want to do this?
(What will it bring into your life? What makes you
enthusiastic about it? How is it in line with your North
Star?)

What resources and support do you already have for
this?
(Count everything! Things you already know, people you
can talk to, customers who want this...)

How do you think you'll feel when you accomplish this?
Be specific!

Off the top of your head, what will this involve?
(*We'll work these details out during map-making.*)

SPECTACULAR THING #4

Why do you want to do this?
*(What will it bring into your life? What makes you
enthusiastic about it? How is it in line with your North
Star?)*

What resources and support do you already have for
this?
*(Count everything! Things you already know, people you
can talk to, customers who want this...)*

How do you think you'll feel when you accomplish this?
Be specific!

Off the top of your head, what will this involve?
(We'll work these details out during map-making.)

GETTING SPECIFIC

Let's make your big list of stuff to do more specific!
What are the areas that really matter to you this year?

What specific changes do you want to make in those areas?

What one-time decision could you make, that will make your year better?
(ex. I'll buy myself fresh flowers every week. Or, I'll post on Instagram daily.)

What habits would make your goals more likely to happen?

REAL MONEY STUFF

What big expenses do you expect to have this year?
(shows, travel, buying equipment, replacing computers,
etc.)

What's the estimated cost?
(Give a number!)

What's your yearly income goal?

What's your sales goal?
(Expenses + Income = Sales Goal)

How can you reach that sales goal?
(How many of what products would you sell? Where?
Try working with different configurations until it feels do-
able.)

Product   *Price*   *Amount I'd need to sell*

WHAT WILL YOU DO TO SELL MORE?

In order to increase sales, you'll need to increase or improve your marketing (see my book, Market Yourself, for step-by-step instructions on making your marketing plan). Your plan may include launches, using tools more consistently or effectively, and introducing new products. Write your ideas or plans for each here.

What will I launch? When?

What tools do I use in my marketing?

What do I need to become more consistent with?

What tool do I want to learn more about? When will I implement that learning?

How can I listen to my customers more?

When will I implement this?

REMEMBER THE THINGS YOU SAID YOU WANTED TO START MEASURING IN THE FIRST SECTION? THIS IS THE PLACE TO GET SPECIFIC!

Fill in your current number and your goal for it (only worry about the areas that matter for YOUR business!).

Email list size:

Goal:

When will I focus on growing this?

Website visits/month:

Goal:

When will I focus on growing this?

Facebook page or group:

Goal:

When will I focus on growing this?

Instagram:

Goal:

When will I focus on growing this?

Products in shop:
Goal:
When I will focus on this?

Twitter/Ravelry group/other:
Goal:
When will I focus on this?

TOOLS AND SUPPORT

What supports your business and your life?
(friends, mentors, books, systems)

What would you like to add to your support system?
(a babysitter, an assistant, a book about marketing, a shop-owner friend)

How much time do you want to spend on your business each week?
(Time you spend building it and improving it, not time you spend working in it.)

How do you spend your time now?
Draw a pie chart or make a list.

How would you like to spend it?

What could you do to change this?

BUSINESS SPECIFICS

What are the shows you want to apply to this year? *(Write in their application date beside it. Go on! Look it up!)*

What are the shops you want to approach this year?

Who is the "gate-keeper" you need to connect with? *(This might be an artist's rep, a magazine editor, a book agent.)*

BREAKING IT DOWN

Now's the time to take your big goals, tiny missions and everything in between and put it on a month. It's ok if you don't have every single to-do from every goal (we'll get that specific in the quarterly map-making, when you're ready to focus on it), but think about it in terms of big projects or current commitments.

On the next pages, list your answers to the following questions under the appropriate month:

What projects are already planned (travel, shows, family stuff)? What projects will be in what months?

What do you want to focus on in what months?

Take your yearly income goal, and break it down by month.

Add in craft shows, and then put their prep in previous months.

JANUARY

FEBRUARY

MARCH

APRIL

MAY

JUNE

JULY

AUGUST

SEPTEMBER

OCTOBER

NOVEMBER

DECEMBER

DARLING! YOU DID IT! YOU SET IN MOTION A MOST-FABULOUS YEAR!

Remember: the BEST way to make all your dreams come true?

* Get clear on what you really want.
* Break it down into do-able steps.
* Tell someone who can hold you gently, non-guiltily accountable.

* Reassess and adjust regularly.

You've done #1 already (yay!) and the next step is to break this into a do-able plan for the next three months, and then put it all in whatever calendar or planner you like to use.

We'll do this via Map Making: First you'll set your goal and focus for the next three months and figure out where you are now in relation to where you want to be. Then, you'll identify the steps along the way (mini-accomplishments) on the way to your goal. Finally, you'll look at every single action you need to take and put it all in a map you can follow for the next 3 months.

IF YOU JUST FINISHED LOOKING AT THE BIG PICTURE, I RECOMMEND YOU TAKE A BREAK BEFORE COMING BACK TO MAP MAKING.

Take a day (or two) to let your big goals and pictures and North Stars sink in. Living with what you want and what you're excited about (and sleeping on it!) will make it easier for you to set one specific goal for the next 3 months.

MAP MAKING

Now that you know what you want to do, it's time to break it down into do-able steps.

I've used a version of this process (before I ever officially wrote it down) to do stuff like quit my day job, get ready for a craft show, pitch and write magazine articles, dream of, plan, and finish my first book, and yeah, even finish this book you hold in your hands! I started leading makers and artists through the process in 2010 and in the years since, it's helped hundreds of small businesses reach their sales goals, quit their day jobs, get published and just have a better summer with their kids.

IT'S A POWERFUL TOOL, BUT IT'S NOT MAGICAL.

You bring the magic and the smarts and a willingness to have FUN with it and the process makes it all a little easier. But your goals actually only happen if you do the work. This process will help you make it much more do-able... but then you have to DO.

This isn't a one-time fix.

In the next few pages we'll break down ONE goal into a plan to reach that goal in about three months. But there are a few things I've learned in the years of using this process:

* You may not need to do everything you plan to do. The goal may come sooner! This is NOT about doing everything on the list, it's about reaching the goal.
* You may realize half the things on the list aren't going to get you to your goal. Stop and reassess and change your list!
* You may not reach your goal because it was just not reasonable. That's ok! If you've moved towards your goal, that's progress! Look at what worked, and do more of that!
* You may not reach your goal, even after doing everything. That's ok! It's all data, to use for making your next map. You now know what doesn't work, so you can try other things that may work.

Many of my students make a new map every quarter (ie, every three months). Sometimes these maps are for different projects, sometimes it's the same goal, stretched over a few maps before they reach it. In other words, all is not lost if you don't reach your goal immediately! Don't give up - keep experimenting, assessing, and adjusting.

I've included enough Map Making worksheets to use them every three months, so you can make a new map as you go through your year.

PICK A GOAL

It's important to pick **a time frame** and **an endpoint** for your map (a goal) at the same time, so the two match up.

WHAT WE'RE LOOKING FOR HERE IS SOMETHING THAT WILL BE A CHALLENGE, BUT DO-ABLE IN 1 OR 3 OR 6 MONTHS.

Big and glorious, but not something that would require 5 years. Yes, you have goals that will take 5 years, so the first step is break it down into a smaller chunk. If everything progressed at a steady pace, where would you be in 1 year? And what's a ¼ of that?

That said, we tend to overestimate what we can do in a day, but underestimate what we can do in a month (or a year), so go ahead and stretch.

Let's look at an example:
Goal: Make 100,000 in sales per year.
Currently make $100.

Let's just guess you can reach this in 3 years (although with focus and dedication, you can certainly do it sooner!).

Let's say we'll double each year: $100,000 in 3, $50,00 in 2 years, $25,000 in one year.

So your goal is $25,000 in sales this year. The fourth quarter is always higher, so let's shoot for $4,000 in sales this quarter, and then more in each following quarter. That's our destination for this map: $4,000 in sales. *(This is only an example! Some businesses will move much more slowly or be more seasonal.)*

So now's the time to look at your Big Wonderful projects from earlier and either pick one of them as your destination for the next 3 months or break them down into a chunk you can do this quarter.

Now, before you really settle in on this goal, let's make sure it's a good fit for a map.

How will you measure it? What metrics will you use?

How will you know you've reached this goal?

If your goal wasn't measurable, how can we make it measurable?

How can you shift it or change it so that it becomes more tangible, more physical?

Now that you have a good, measurable goal, let's ground yourself in where you are right now.

Look at some of those metrics that you're going to use for your goal-reaching. What do they look like right now?

This is the time to get *honest*, but not mean.

Where you are is exactly where you should be. You aren't behind. You aren't slow.

As long as you beat yourself up for not being there already, you won't have the energy to focus on getting there.

TRUST ME, IT'S NOT TOO LATE.

Fill out the following worksheet to address where you want to go and where you are right now. You may have already done this in the earlier worksheets, but this is in relation to this specific goal, so don't skip it!

WHERE YOU ARE +
WHERE YOU WANT TO
BE

WHERE DO YOU WANT TO GO?

1. What's your time frame?
   What's your goal? Write it in the form of a sentence.

In _ _ _ _ months I will

_ _.

2. What metrics will you use to measure your goal? *Money earned? Items created? Items sold? Tasks completed?*

3. How will you know you've reached your goal? Use specifics (like: number + metric).

WHERE YOU ARE:

1. Using the above metrics (whichever ones you chose), where are you now?
    Get specific! Do some math, check some facts, and take the time to do it now.

2. Notice any feelings or thoughts that come up as you research and write down your current status. Don't censor yourself + write down what you noticed (if you need more space, write in your journal or insert a blank sheet of paper).

THE FIRST STEP TO GETTING THERE: GET EMOTIONALLY SPECIFIC

We're going to address something a little deeper than just setting goals and making To-Do lists, because you know how to do that already.

I'm going to ask you to think (and write) about your feelings + to really pay attention to how you react to the steps of the entire guide.

> *(Side-note: I use to think this wasn't my thing, and I would skip it when I came to it; but eventually I realized it was all that ignoring-how-I-feel-about it-ness that was getting in my way. I'm a child of two Marines, so I know how to power through. But I assure you: this paying-attention thing is much easier on you, your focus and your creative energy.)*

CLOSE YOUR EYES. TAKE THREE DEEP BREATHS.

NOW PICTURE YOURSELF AT THE END OF YOUR MAP. YOUR GOAL HAS BEEN REACHED.

What does that feel like? Pay attention to both your emotions + how it feels in your body.

Write down, as specifically as you can, how you feel (*not how you think you should feel*) when you imagine this success.

(I promise, we're going to cover tangible actions in the next steps, but I want you to do this first, so you can make sure you're actually looking forward to the change that will come with success. I've found I often feel different than I thought I would at the beginning of a project, or that some un-looked-at feelings crop up and derail me mid-way).

LOOK FOR MILE MARKERS

Now that you know where you are and where you want to go, it's time to look at the path ahead of you.

Let's focus on the things that will happen on your way to your goal.

These are not To-Do items (the stuff you have to do to get there), these are the events and mini-goals you'll reach on your path. I call these mile markers, because they help you measure your progress. They are mini-successes!

Looking for these ahead of time can help keep you encouraged as you move forward. Better than that, they'll keep you on the right path and will keep you from straying or getting distracted.

Best yet, they are super-simple to make.

Using the following worksheet, list ten mile markers that will show up on your path.

YES, TEN!

Why?

Because it's too easy to get overwhelmed by the Big Goal, the Destination, and not notice all the other little measurable changes that will happen first. And often, you can't control everything that happens in your path. A mile-marker is a thing that occurs because of the work you've done, and often takes a lot more work or doing than you anticipated!

Make sure all ten items can be *measured.* The metrics might be different than your Big Goal, but they should definitely be measurable!

WHAT WILL HAPPEN BEFORE YOU REACH YOUR GOAL, THAT WILL LET YOU KNOW YOU'RE ON YOUR WAY THERE?

(Example: If your destination is to do your first craft show, then getting accepted is a mile-marker. Finding the application, taking good pictures, and actually applying are all to-dos. The mile-marker is sometimes out of your control, but the to-dos are always within your control. Something you can do in a a few hours.)

MILE MARKERS
(LIST 10!)

GET TO THE MILE MARKERS

Now we're really digging in, friend.

We're going to make a ginormous list of all the things you'll actually do on your path to your Big Goal.
But before you get started, ignore the Big Goal (for now!) and focus on how you can get to the mile markers. Focus on the *mile markers* and you'll get to the Big Goal. I promise!

We're going to start by having you list 50 real, physical To-Dos. But pay attention! Write down only actions that are related to your goal, do NOT write down all the stuff you think you need to do in your business!

One of the main benefits of Map Making is that it helps you separate general "should-dos" that are floating around your head, from the "actually applicable to my goals" To Dos, so that you can focus on what matters (and ignore the rest).

RIGHT NOW, BEFORE YOU READ
FURTHER, GO TO THE NEXT PAGE
AND START WRITING DOWN TO-DOS.

DON'T COME BACK UNTIL YOU'RE RUNNING OUT OF STEAM.

If you're slowing down and can't think of more items, get very very specific.

Look at a mile marker and list five things that will get you there (every mile marker doesn't have to have five To-Dos, but this will help you generate more ideas).

DONE WITH YOUR LIST?

Hold on! Take a breath! Don't get overwhelmed! You're listing all the specific steps, but this just means you will also get the pleasure of marking off all those things!

As you move through your mile markers, you'll realize that some things on your list either *don't need doing* or they don't make the kind of impact you had hoped.

Really, you won't have to do everything on this list. Your goal may happen before you've done them all. Or you may realize they are not as related to your goal as you thought. You are allowed to shift and change and delete things at any point.

But yes, you DO need to write down 50 things.

50 AMAZING TO-DOS

REARRANGE THAT LIST

Your list of 50 is *really* fabulous. You could probably start working on it today, right?

But the thing is, most actions (especially in a business!) provide the most impact when you line them up like dominoes. For example: it doesn't make sense to try to list a new product until you've taken its photo.

This is a journey we're making a map for, right? Some steps need to come before the others.

If you approach it willy-nilly, you're gonna get stuck. And probably discouraged. And you won't be able to use the pretty maps to make sense of it all... so don't skip this step!

TAKE YOUR MILE MARKERS AND REARRANGE THEM IN COMMONSENSE ORDER.

What is closest to you right now? What is closest to your goal?

Put your Mile Markers in order from Today to Goal.

NOW, LIST YOUR TO-DOS (YOUR LIST OF 50) UNDER THE MILE MARKERS THEY MATCH UP WITH.

What needs to come first? Second? What's one of the last things that will happen before you get to that mile marker?

Some To-Dos might be more general, so go on and put them in their own general group.

You can use the following page to help you rearrange.

TAKE AS MUCH SPACE AS YOU NEED AND DON'T WORRY ABOUT MAKING IT MESSY!

REARRANGE!

MAKE THAT MAP

Now for the fun!
We're going to take everything you've done so far and make it all more visual and *visible* and fun.

Pick a template

In the next few pages, you've got a Fairyland map and a CraftyLand map. You can use the one you like, or draw your own on the next blank page.

Fill it in

Pick an end point and write your Big Goal (your destination) on it!

Take your rearranged mile markers and write them onto the map.

> *(Prettify tip: to get them evenly spaced, put in the first marker, then the last, then the middle, then fill in the ones that come between.)*

Pay attention to which mile marker will come first and which ones will be closer to your end goal.

IF YOU WRITE BIG, YOU MIGHT WANT TO TAKE THE MAPS AND JOIN THEM TOGETHER TO MAKE ONE LONGER OR BIGGER MAP.

If you have the space, you can write your individual To-Dos on your map, in the space between where you are and the next mile marker. (Don't write in all your To-Dos, just the ones you need to do for the next section.)

MAKE IT EVEN PRETTIER!

Cut out any of the extras, color them in and put them in the empty spaces! Maybe you want the castle at your endpoint or a dragon guarding a moat. Maybe you'll have to build a bridge over a paint spill. Or perhaps you'll take a detour when something unexpected comes up.

Why bother making it visual?

If you're a visual person, having a map that you can see and reference and move down can help you stay motivated as you work. It will also make something vague and ephemeral much more tangible.

(If you're more of a words person than a visual person, you may get more out of keeping the written list in front of you.)

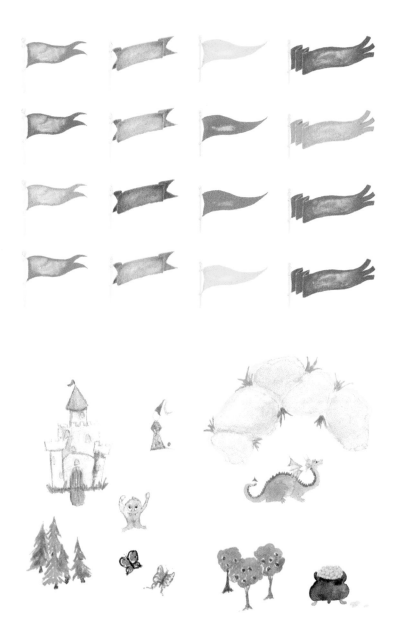

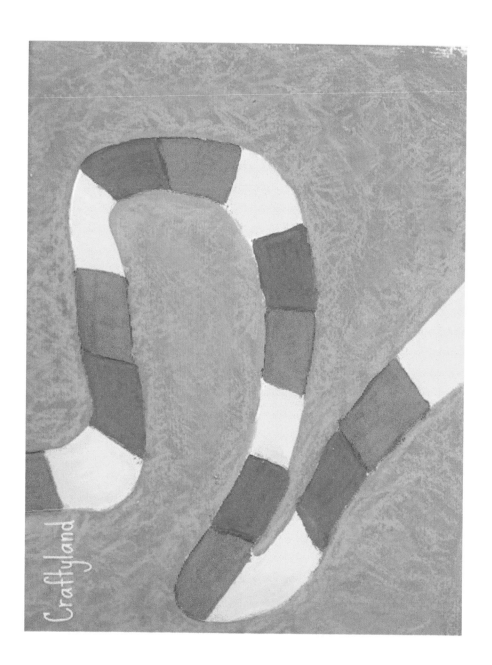

Craftyland

DRAW YOUR OWN MAP

BONUS TIPS FOR USING YOUR MAP

This map-making process can be whatever you find most useful.

For some people, the simple exercise is enough to propel them forward. All they really use is the list of mile markers and To-Dos. For others, they'll hang the map up and check in from time to time. Yet others will make the map-checking and list-marking a daily or weekly part of their business.

EXPERIMENT AND FIND WHAT WORKS BEST FOR YOU!

Use it weekly: at the end (or beginning) of your week, revisit your list and note what you need to do next to reach your next mile marker. Look at your map and write in the next steps (and mark off the ones you've done).

Make it a game! Use any of the "extras" as a game piece and move them down the path as you progress towards your goal. When you come up against detours or struggles, make them cute by adding in a funny boulder or cranky tree right on your map!

Don't focus on the Big List. As soon as you're done making your map, stop looking at the big list. Instead, look at the tasks directly in front of you. Turn your focus to the next mile marker and work exclusively on that.

WHAT'S NEXT

DUDE! YOU DID IT!

You have gotten clarity about the business you really want, you set goals and you broke at least one goal down into do-able steps! You've taken what was a vague-ish thought and it turned it into actionable steps.

THAT'S AWESOME AND DESERVES CELEBRATION! YAY!

But what comes next is even more important: You have to do the work. And then reassess and do more work.

Here's what to do next:

1. Transfer the very next To Dos (the ones related to your first Mile Marker) to your schedule or planner. I've talked more about the tools and planners I use here: https://taraswiger.com/podcast134/

2. Don't wait until the end of the quarter or year to see if your dreams came true or if you're taking the right actions. Reassess every month (using the following pages!) and adjust course!

3. At the end of the quarter, review your map. Did you reach the goal? Why not? What worked? What didn't?
4. Make a new map! Maybe you want to work towards the same goal, or maybe you want or need to focus on a different area. If a project or goal feels too overwhelming, make a map for it!

In my online community, The Starship, we make new maps every quarter, so I've included the Map Making worksheets after every 3 monthly review worksheets. Over the last 6 years of leading hundreds of makers and artists towards reaching their goals, I've learned that this amount of time is just perfect for narrow focus - not so long that you forget about it and not so short that you can't see major progress.

But remember: Use this in the way that works for you! If something comes up that changes your life or business the week after you made a map, make a new one! If you change your focus, make a new one! Even though your clarity is awesome, don't get attached to it. You and your business and your life will change a lot in the next year. You'll be happier and more fulfilled if you reassess and change your goals to fit your changed life.

And in six months or a year, come back and do the whole thing again!

You can find more resources, examples and advice at TaraSwiger.com and on my podcast, Explore Your Enthusiasm.

I'm wishing you a successful, enthusiastic year!

MONTHLY
REVIEWS

THE MONTHLY
REASSESSMENT

REVIEWING THE LAST
MONTH

MONTH:

What went smoothly?

What surprised you? What did you learn?

What to-do, mile-marker, or goal do you need to adjust (or let go of) based on what just happened?

What goal (big or small) did you reach this month?

What was your gross income for this month?

How does that compare to your goal?

Why the difference?

What might you try differently next month?

`

How did your North Star show up for you this month?

NEXT MONTH PLOTTING

Next month is:

What expenses are coming up this month?

How much I need to make:

How much I want to make:

How might that work:

What projects need your attention this month?

What are you enthusiastic about this month?

How do you want to feel as you move toward your goals this month?

What to-dos and mile markers from your map fit in this month?

How will you move closer to your map's destination?

How will you bring the qualities of your North Star into the next month?

THE MONTHLY REASSESSMENT

MONTH:

What went smoothly?

What surprised you? What did you learn?

What to-do, mile-marker, or goal do you need to adjust (or let go of) based on what just happened?

What goal (big or small) did you reach this month?

What was your gross income for this month?

How does that compare to your goal?

Why the difference?

What might you try differently next month?

How did your North Star show up for you this month?

NEXT MONTH PLOTTING

Next month is:

What expenses are coming up this month?

How much I need to make:

How much I want to make:

How might that work:

What projects need your attention this month?

What are you enthusiastic about this month?

How do you want to feel as you move toward your goals this month?

What to-dos and mile markers from your map fit in this month?

How will you move closer to your map's destination?

How can you bring the qualities of your North Star into your next month?

THE MONTHLY REASSESSMENT

REVIEWING THE LAST
MONTH

MONTH:

What went smoothly?

What surprised you? What did you learn?

What to-do, mile-marker, or goal do you need to adjust (or let go of) based on what just happened?

What goal (big or small) did you reach this month?

What was your gross income for this month?

How does that compare to your goal?

Why the difference?

What might you try differently next month?

How did your North Star show up for you this month?

Next month is:

What expenses are coming up this month?

How much I need to make:

How much I want to make:

How might that work:

What projects need your attention this month?

What are you enthusiastic about this month?

How do you want to feel as you move toward your goals this month?

What to-dos and mile markers from your map fit in this month?

How will you move closer to your map's destination?

How can you bring the qualities of your North Star into your next month?

MAP MAKING

If you want to make another map for the next 3 months, here are the Map Making worksheets!.

Use them now, or use them later!

WHERE YOU WANT TO BE + WHERE YOU ARE

WHERE DO YOU WANT TO GO?

1. What's your time frame?
   What's your goal? Write it in the form of a sentence.

In _ _ _ _ months I will

_ _.

2. What metrics will you use to measure your goal? Money earned? Items created? Items sold? Tasks completed?

3. How will you know you've reached your goal? Use specifics (like: number + metric).

WHERE YOU ARE:

1. Using the above metrics (whichever ones you chose), where are you now?
   Get specific! Do some math, check some facts, and take the time to do it now.

2. Notice any feelings or thoughts that come up as you research and write down your current status. Don't censor yourself + write down what you noticed (if you need more space, write in your journal or insert a blank sheet of paper).

MILE MARKERS
(LIST 10!)

50 AMAZING TO-DOS

REARRANGE!

.

DRAW YOUR OWN MAP

THE MONTHLY
REASSESSMENT

REVIEWING THE LAST
MONTH

MONTH:

What went smoothly?

What surprised you? What did you learn?

What to-do, mile-marker, or goal do you need to adjust (or let go of) based on what just happened?

What goal (big or small) did you reach this month?

What was your gross income for this month?

How does that compare to your goal?

Why the difference?

What might you try differently next month?

How did your North Star show up for you this month?

NEXT MONTH PLOTTING
Next month is:

What expenses are coming up this month?

How much I need to make:

How much I want to make:

How might that work:

What projects need your attention this month?

What are you enthusiastic about this month?

How do you want to feel as you move toward your goals this month?

What to-dos and mile markers from your map fit in this month?

How will you move closer to your map's destination?

How can you bring the qualities of your North Star into your next month?

THE MONTHLY
REASSESSMENT

REVIEWING THE LAST
MONTH

MONTH:

What went smoothly?

What surprised you? What did you learn?

What to-do, mile-marker, or goal do you need to adjust
(or let go of) based on what just happened?

What goal (big or small) did you reach this month?

What was your gross income for this month?

How does that compare to your goal?

Why the difference?

What might you try differently next month?

How did your North Star show up for you this month?

NEXT MONTH PLOTTING

Next month is:

What expenses are coming up this month?

How much I need to make:

How much I want to make:

How might that work:

What projects need your attention this month?

What are you enthusiastic about this month?

How do you want to feel as you move toward your goals this month?

What to-dos and mile markers from your map fit in this month?

How will you move closer to your map's destination?

How can you bring the qualities of your North Star into your next month?

THE MONTHLY
REASSESSMENT

MONTH:

What went smoothly?

What surprised you? What did you learn?

What to-do, mile-marker, or goal do you need to adjust (or let go of) based on what just happened?

What goal (big or small) did you reach this month?

What was your gross income for this month?

How does that compare to your goal?

Why the difference?

What might you try differently next month?

How did your North Star show up for you this month?

NEXT MONTH PLOTTING

Next month is:

What expenses are coming up this month?

How much I need to make:

How much I want to make:

How might that work:

What projects need your attention this month?

What are you enthusiastic about this month?

How do you want to feel as you move toward your goals this month?

What to-dos and mile markers from your map fit in this month?

How will you move closer to your map's destination?

How can you bring the qualities of your North Star into your next month?

MAP MAKING

If you want to make another map for the next 3 months, here are the Map Making worksheets!

Use them now, or use them later!

WHERE YOU WANT TO BE + WHERE YOU ARE

WHERE DO YOU WANT TO GO?

1. What's your time frame?
   What's your goal? Write it in the form of a sentence.

In _ _ _ _ months I will

_ _

2. What metrics will you use to measure your goal? Money earned? Items created? Items sold? Tasks completed?

3. How will you know you've reached your goal? Use specifics (like: number + metric).

WHERE YOU ARE:

1. Using the above metrics (whichever ones you chose), where are you now?
Get specific! Do some math, check some facts, and take the time to do it now.

2. Notice any feelings or thoughts that come up as you research and write down your current status. Don't censor yourself + write down what you noticed (if you need more space, write in your journal or insert a blank sheet of paper).

MILE MARKERS
(LIST 10!)

50 AMAZING TO-DOS

REARRANGE!

DRAW YOUR OWN MAP

THE MONTHLY
REASSESSMENT

REVIEWING THE LAST MONTH

MONTH:

What went smoothly?

What surprised you? What did you learn?

What to-do, mile-marker, or goal do you need to adjust (or let go of) based on what just happened?

What goal (big or small) did you reach this month?

What was your gross income for this month?

How does that compare to your goal?

Why the difference?

What might you try differently next month?

How did your North Star show up for you this month?

NEXT MONTH PLOTTING
Next month is:

What expenses are coming up this month?

How much I need to make:

How much I want to make:

How might that work:

What projects need your attention this month?

What are you enthusiastic about this month?

How do you want to feel as you move toward your goals this month?

What to-dos and mile markers from your map fit in this month?

How will you move closer to your map's destination?

How can you bring the qualities of your North Star into your next month?

THE MONTHLY
REASSESSMENT
REVIEWING THE LAST
MONTH

MONTH:

What went smoothly?

What surprised you? What did you learn?

What to-do, mile-marker, or goal do you need to adjust (or let go of) based on what just happened?

What goal (big or small) did you reach this month?

What was your gross income for this month?

How does that compare to your goal?

Why the difference?

What might you try differently next month?

How did your North Star show up for you this month?

NEXT MONTH PLOTTING
Next month is:

What expenses are coming up this month?

How much I need to make:

How much I want to make:

How might that work:

What projects need your attention this month?

What are you enthusiastic about this month?

How do you want to feel as you move toward your goals this month?

What to-dos and mile markers from your map fit in this month?

How will you move closer to your map's destination?

How can you bring the qualities of your North Star into your next month?

THE MONTHLY
REASSESSMENT

MONTH:

What went smoothly?

What surprised you? What did you learn?

What to-do, mile-marker, or goal do you need to adjust
(or let go of) based on what just happened?

What goal (big or small) did you reach this month?

What was your gross income for this month?

How does that compare to your goal?

Why the difference?

What might you try differently next month?

How did your North Star show up for you this month?

NEXT MONTH PLOTTING

Next month is:

What expenses are coming up this month?

How much I need to make:

How much I want to make:

How might that work:

What projects need your attention this month?

What are you enthusiastic about this month?

How do you want to feel as you move toward your goals this month?

What to-dos and mile markers from your map fit in this month?

How will you move closer to your map's destination?

How can you bring the qualities of your North Star into your next month?

MAP MAKING

If you want to make another map for the next 3 months, here are the Map Making worksheets!

Use them now, or use them later!

WHERE YOU WANT TO BE + WHERE YOU ARE

WHERE DO YOU WANT TO GO?

1. What's your time frame?
   What's your goal? Write it in the form of a sentence.

In ____ months I will

----

2. What metrics will you use to measure your goal? Money earned? Items created? Items sold? Tasks completed?

3. How will you know you've reached your goal? Use specifics (like: number + metric).

WHERE YOU ARE:

1. Using the above metrics (whichever ones you chose), where are you now?
Get specific! Do some math, check some facts, and take the time to do it now.

2. Notice any feelings or thoughts that come up as you research and write down your current status. Don't censor yourself + write down what you noticed (if you need more space, write in your journal or insert a blank sheet of paper).

MILE MARKERS
(LIST 10!)

50 AMAZING TO-DOS

REARRANGE!

DRAW YOUR OWN MAP

THE MONTHLY
REASSESSMENT

REVIEWING THE LAST
MONTH

MONTH:

What went smoothly?

What surprised you? What did you learn?

What to-do, mile-marker, or goal do you need to adjust
(or let go of) based on what just happened?

What goal (big or small) did you reach this month?

What was your gross income for this month?

How does that compare to your goal?

Why the difference?

What might you try differently next month?

How did your North Star show up for you this month?

NEXT MONTH PLOTTING
Next month is:

What expenses are coming up this month?

How much I need to make:

How much I want to make:

How might that work:

What projects need your attention this month?

What are you enthusiastic about this month?

How do you want to feel as you move toward your goals this month?

What to-dos and mile markers from your map fit in this month?

How will you move closer to your map's destination?

How can you bring the qualities of your North Star into your next month?

THE MONTHLY
REASSESSMENT
REVIEWING THE LAST
MONTH

MONTH:

What went smoothly?

What surprised you? What did you learn?

What to-do, mile-marker, or goal do you need to adjust (or let go of) based on what just happened?

What goal (big or small) did you reach this month?

What was your gross income for this month?

How does that compare to your goal?

Why the difference?

What might you try differently next month?

How did your North Star show up for you this month?

NEXT MONTH PLOTTING

Next month is:

What expenses are coming up this month?

How much I need to make:

How much I want to make:

How might that work:

What projects need your attention this month?

What are you enthusiastic about this month?

How do you want to feel as you move toward your goals this month?

What to-dos and mile markers from your map fit in this month?

How will you move closer to your map's destination?

How can you bring the qualities of your North Star into your next month?

THE MONTHLY
REASSESSMENT

MONTH:

What went smoothly?

What surprised you? What did you learn?

What to-do, mile-marker, or goal do you need to adjust
(or let go of) based on what just happened?

What goal (big or small) did you reach this month?

What was your gross income for this month?

How does that compare to your goal?

Why the difference?

What might you try differently next month?

How did your North Star show up for you this month?

NEXT MONTH PLOTTING
Next month is:
What expenses are coming up this month?

How much I need to make:

How much I want to make:

How might that work:

What projects need your attention this month?

What are you enthusiastic about this month?

How do you want to feel as you move toward your goals this month?

What to-dos and mile markers from your map fit in this month?

How will you move closer to your map's destination?

How can you bring the qualities of your North Star into your next month?

YOU DID IT!

You've figured out what you want and worked on it and reassessed and worked some more for a whole year! Yaaaay!

REMEMBER: YOU ARE NOT ALONE IN THIS!

I would LOVE to see your map and hear about your experiences. Share your maps on Twitter or Instagram, using the hashtag #mapyourbusiness.

If you enjoyed the map-making process and feel like you need more accountability, support, and some help with the specifics of exploring your business (marketing, profitability, and time management), check out the Starship. It's a metaphorical ship full of very real classes, help from me, and the smartest handmade biz owners ready to advise + support you. You can find at TaraSwiger.com/starshipbiz.

ACKNOWLEDGEMENTS

My first and biggest sloppy thank you kisses go to Jay, who laid out this book, put up with my will-it-ever-be-done freakouts, and makes my whole life possible. I love you.

Jessica Cook edited, encouraged and researched the ins and outs of making this book happen. Thank you for this and for everything, Jess.

Thank you to the Starship Captains who pretty much forced me to make this with your requests for it, your knowledge about publishing, and your votes on everything from the name to the contents.

Thank you to my Patrons, who make my books, podcasts, and videos possible.

As always, my Mom, my Dad and my Cathi are responsible for shaping me into the kind of person who can write a book and run a business. I'm forever grateful for your unconditional love, encouragement, and confidence.

ABOUT THE AUTHOR

Tara Swiger is an author, maker and Starship Captain. She leads makers and artists in becoming their own best business advisor through her books, weekly podcast, and workshops online and around the world.

Her first book, Market Yourself (Cooperative Press, 2012), is a workbook that guides handmade businesses through creating their first marketing plan, by identifying their message and finding their best buyers.

You can find weekly podcast episodes, online workshops, and more books at TaraSwiger.com.

Lightning Source UK Ltd.
Milton Keynes UK
UKOW06f1358230317

297351UK00014BA/97/P